The Stars
that Knew you

ALSO BY LYRA WREN

The Lost Girls:
*a poetry collection on girlhood,
grief and growing up*

The Stars
that Knew you

LYRA WREN

Indianapolis, Indiana

Lyra Wren
@poetrybylyra
linktr.ee/poetrybylyra

ISBN: 979-8-9915591-0-2

Edited by Maddie Portune

Cover and Book Design by Keller Makemson
@kmakemson.design
kmakemson.com

Dedicated to *the girls*.

Being your older sister
is one of the greatest joys in my life.
I've got your back and
I'll always be by your side.

My sister and I were lying side by side
beneath the moonlight when she softly said,

"If you told me the stars knew you
by name, I would believe you."

"I think if they knew anyone's name,
it would be yours." I replied.

She wrinkled her nose in confusion
before quietly asking, "Why?"

"Because all I ever do is speak of you."

Contents

Section I: Solis

The Latin Word for Sun.

The sun burns brightly for all to see,
shining through me with protection and ferocity.

I was born at the center
and I'm meant to lead the way.

To teach by example
every single day.

I am the older sister
and I tether us together.

LYRA WREN

I think you called to me
long before you existed on earth.

When you were born,
I saw this pink, screaming thing.
Someone that should have been foreign
but was as familiar as my own heartbeat.
We belonged to each other and I knew you.
I don't know how but I *knew* you.

For two years, I existed as an only child
but I can hardly remember a time
that you weren't in my life.
I think I just waited.
I waited to be a full person
until the day you arrived.

LYRA WREN

My mother held me close and whispered to me
that after my sisters were born,
I would always leave my room and
fall asleep outside of their closed doors.

I was only three and already,
I had taken them under my wing.
Maybe it's an innate trait of the eldest daughter
to watch over their sisters as their protector.

Whether it's in our dna or the way we are raised,
it becomes our job to keep them safe.

THE STARS THAT KNEW YOU

What was mine and
what was yours began to blur
until the line was so grey
I forgot there was ever
a mark between us in the first place.

LYRA WREN

The light switch is down the basement stairs.
A place where shadows move and stir
into monstrous things.

If we wanted to play there,
we needed to go down but—
I'm scared of the dark, I thought.

"I'm scared of the dark," my little sister said out loud.

My heartbeat echoed in my ears.
A gripping fear lurked in my chest.
But I took a deep breath and made my way down,
because my job was to be scared
so one day she could be brave on her own.

THE STARS THAT KNEW YOU

When she had a bad dream I lifted my sheets,
letting her crawl into my bed.
I promised her that nothing could get her here.
"You're safe with me. It's a fortress built of blankets,"
I'd whisper.

I'd tell her stories about the stars
and make up my own constellations.
And as she drifted to sleep
I'd promise that she'd always be safe with me.

The youngest is complaining
about growing pains,
an unforgiving ache in her limbs.

My mother assures her it is natural.
"It just means you are getting older."

I don't know yet that in a few years
the baby fat will have faded from her cheeks
and she will be taller than me.

Growing pains were supposed to be in my past,
but a sudden pang shoots through my chest.
She's getting older right in front of my eyes
and it makes my heart hurt unlike anything else.

THE STARS THAT KNEW YOU

I taught my little sister how to ride a bike
on the path behind our backyard.
She made me promise that I'd hold on to her
and that I wouldn't let her fall.

I was little too but I felt this pride
that she wanted me to guide her.
We tried over and over again
because she was so determined to ride it.

There must have been a last time
that I let go of her before she was on her own.
I'm not a mother but I felt an echo then,
the tragedy they must feel knowing you have grown.

I'm sorry to my little sisters
for all the times I pushed you away.
Greeting you with angst and rage
and saying no when you asked me to play.

I met you with cruelty
where there should have been love.
I made you feel lower
when I should have held you up.

I wish I had been a better sister to you,
never making you feel attacked.
But you are older now
and I cannot take it back.

THE STARS THAT KNEW YOU

I have a scar on the palm of my hand
from when my little sister bit me.
A pale crescent ring in the shape of her teeth.

Little sisters learn to bite
when their big sisters pick a fight.
Eventually, I thought it would fade but it stayed
and looking back I'm happy it did.
Because for the rest of my life,
I will carry a permanent reminder of her stubborn fire.

My parents used to tell that because I was older,
I needed to set an example for my younger siblings.
I wasn't allowed to fail but I did.
So many times, I did.

Each time they insisted
that I needed to do better,
show them how to be better.

But what of me? I'm a child, too.
I'm too young to bear that weight
on top of my tiny shoulders.
Nobody is perfect.
Not even the older sisters.

I'm your big sister
and it's my job to make everything okay.
But the times I can't
we'll walk the path together and
I'll hold your hand the entire way.

LYRA WREN

I told you about the stars
and I told the stars about you.
You have a lot in common, you see.

There's a twinkle in the sky
that's reflected in your eyes.
You shine so brightly and remind me
of why I love being alive.

A thread of connection flows
through my chest.
Something ancient and unseen.
Our sisterhood is everlasting,
we will remain together for all eternity.

THE STARS THAT KNEW YOU

I didn't know what to do
with the responsibility
that was laid at my feet.
I needed to be perfect because
they were looking up to me.

I could not make a mistake
without thinking that
I was in the wrong.
I was growing too but
I had to be strong.

When you get older
your parents will ask you
to take off that mask.

But I learned from them
that to be vulnerable and imperfect
is a terrifying task.

I want to be their shield,
taking every blow.
If I could protect them
from the cruelty of this world
I would, without hesitation.

I wish to carry their burdens
even though I have my own.
But shadowing a seed
will ensure it never grows.

So even though I don't want to,
I'll take a step back.
Knowing they must face their pain
in pursuit of their own path.

THE STARS THAT KNEW YOU

As an older sister, it felt like my job to be the protector.
So when I was drowning in my depression,
I didn't reach for you because it didn't seem to matter.

There were days everything felt bleak
but still, I cried all alone.
Keeping quiet when I suffered because
I thought my tears meant I was weak.

When we got older, you scolded me and said
"We should shoulder this burden together."
And I had to admit that maybe I was wrong.
Being vulnerable with the people you love,
that's what it means to be strong.

LYRA WREN

"Why don't you just say *sister*?
Why do you always add the *little*?"

But how do I begin to explain
how much the *little* means to me?
That it means you are something precious
and I would protect you with my life.
That I would fight with claws and teeth
just to make sure you are thriving.

That I hope you come to me
whenever you are sad or need support.
Because I'm your older sister
and I'll always hold that close to my heart.

THE STARS THAT KNEW YOU

The youngest is moving to a new place today.
One that is hundreds of miles away.
I hugged her before she could leave,
clinging to her like she used to cling to me.

I wanted to beg her to stay
so I didn't have to face this change.
But my pride for her kept me quiet.

"Stay safe," I said instead and then I hesitated.

We rarely exchanged the words because
we all just knew them to be true
but I still said, "I'll love you for as long
as the stars sit up in the night sky."

"So forever?" she asked with a smile.

"For the rest of my life and then some."

LYRA WREN

She's grown up now in front of me
and to others she may look mature.
But when we are together, I see her childish grin
and I know she's still my goofy little sister.

THE STARS THAT KNEW YOU

Watching your little sisters grow up
is both pride and pain filled.
We used to live in the same house
but now I have not seen you in weeks.
And I can't remember the last time
that you really needed me.

Memory lane is saturated in last times
and it's a path I've walked many nights.
I remember you used to look up to me
but as you grew, I found myself
looking up to you too.

Even though you've come into your own
and you'll be moving far away from home.
Just know, I'll always carry you close to me
and you will never truly be alone.

Section II: Lunae

The Latin Word for Moon.

The sun may have come first
but I am the girl who comes after.

Though my light gleams more gently,
my strength pulls the ocean waves right to me.

I had a leader to follow
who showed me how to shine.

I am the little sister
but I am just as mighty.

LYRA WREN

I wonder how many souls
wanted to be your little sister.
How many tried to breathe
life into our mother's womb?

But I think my soul must have known
that we were meant to be family.
I imagine it warmed with familiarity
and sighed in relief as it said,
"There you are. I've been looking for you."

I snuggle up in my blanket cocoon.
Comfortable in knowing my sister
is just across our shared room.

I fall asleep to the sound of our laughter
every single night. It's the sweetest sound
and my favorite kind of lullaby.

LYRA WREN

I remember when we were small,
we asked if you could read to us.
You were older than me but just barely
and you sounded out the words so slowly.
You could hardly connect the line
but we listened to you intently every single time.

Long after I learned to read on my own,
I'd still come to you with a book in hand.
There is love in the way you speak
and the worlds you created for me
were more special than I ever could have dreamed.

THE STARS THAT KNEW YOU

You tease me all the time
and you're always picking fights.

But the same fingers that pull my hair,
will minutes later weave a braid right there.
A silent apology instead of just saying sorry.

You breathe cruelty and kindness
with an ease I understand.
Siblings are just like that
a contradiction of closeness and distance.

LYRA WREN

When I was little
I wanted to play follow the leader
but instead you turned me away.
Yelling at me when I wanted to spend time with you
and saying no when I asked if I could stay.

Maybe being bullied by your older sibling
is some sort of birthright.
But did it have to be that way?
Did we always have to fight?

As the years have passed,
our screaming matches
have softened into teasing.

But I sort of miss those times
and it's the strangest feeling.

THE STARS THAT KNEW YOU

Being the oldest is hard
but it's tough being younger, too.
People don't really think about
what the little sisters go through.

Our first ten years of outfits
are all hand-me-down clothes.
We have no firsts and all we own
are empty baby books.

In games, we play the role
our older sister selects.
Playing the boy Barbies even though
we wanted to be the princess.

Comparison is something we can't avoid
so we constantly hear, *Why can't you be like her?*
When all we want is to be ourselves
instead of being our sister.

LYRA WREN

The middle children, so often forgotten,
are the glue that holds us together.
I want to grab you by the shoulders and shake you.
Remind you that you matter.

There would be no *us* without you
and I would be lost if you were gone.
You are both the older and younger sister.
The middle bond that makes us strong.

THE STARS THAT KNEW YOU

You've been here since the beginning
and you know me like no other.

You're my built-in best friend, my protector
and a second mother.
I will never know what it is to be alone
and I am forever grateful.
That I got to grow up beside you
from the moment I was in the cradle.

I wonder if only children are lonely
but when I ask, they usually shrug and say
not really.

It makes sense, usually you don't miss
what you've never known.
But somehow if you weren't there,
if you had never existed at all.
I know your absence would hang heavy.

Emptiness would linger over my shoulder.
A lack of love that would have
carried the ease of an exhale.

THE STARS THAT KNEW YOU

Loneliness lingered over my shoulder
pressing in on all sides of me.
Physically, I was rarely alone
but I never seemed to fit in anywhere.

Until my sister carved a sense of belonging for me
in the space right beside her.
I knew with certainty then
that no matter where I strayed,
that safety and comfort she gave me
would never go away.

LYRA WREN

I often wonder how my older sister survived
without an older sister of her own.
Who did she go to when she was alone
and desperately needing some advice?

Who peeled apart her oranges to share?
Making sure to give her the bigger half
to show her that they care.

She holds the weight of the world
but still, she listens to my problems
and takes them on fiercely.
But I cannot help but wonder
if she ever felt lonely when she hid away
without a shoulder to cry on.

She never had a built-in playmate
or a sister to be her first friend.
She had to learn it all on her own
and I'm still not sure how she did it.

THE STARS THAT KNEW YOU

If I close my eyes,
I can almost pretend that
my older sister is still playing a video game
and I am still watching.
Pondering the solutions
while she sits there sulking.

I remember the time she looked at me
curiosity filling her gaze.
"Why do you like watching me, wouldn't you rather play?"

"You wouldn't get it," I say with a secretive smile.
"You're the oldest. It's only natural that I watch you."

She was quiet for a moment before she admitted.
"You aren't the only one. I watch you, too."

Maybe that's part of getting older.
We begin to admire each other.
We become both the watcher and the dancer.

LYRA WREN

To my older sister,

I love you to death even when we fight.
Even those times you chased me around
with the kitchen knife.

You picked on me a lot, that's true.
But you were always around when I needed you.

You hugged me after my first breakup
and wiped the tears from my eyes.
Turning on my favorite TV show
even though it's one you despise.

The first one to wish me a happy birthday
right when the clock strikes twelve.
I never have to be anxious about who I am
because I know we can just be ourselves.

So remember that even when we bicker,
I know we can still lean on each other
because you are my older sister.

THE STARS THAT KNEW YOU

"Do you think we would be friends
if we weren't born as sisters?"
I asked my older sister with my chin tucked into my knees.

"I don't know," she answered honestly,
squinting at the sky.
Looking for the meteor shower
we were promised that night.
"We're very different people so maybe not."

I sighed even though I thought she was right.
We barely had the same interests and
our friend groups couldn't be more different.

I glanced at her when she quietly continued.
"But I'd like to think we would have found each other.
That our souls would be drawn together
no matter what role we played."

We both gasped in joy when a shooting star
marked a line in the night sky.
Silently, I wished that we would meet again
in every single lifetime.

LYRA WREN

I looked up to you with starry eyes.
Coming to you when I was lost
and desperately needing some advice.

You were my guiding light,
teaching me right from wrong.
You held my hand through the good and bad
showing me what it meant to be strong.

I don't know what I'd do without you
and I just want to be clear:
that even though I'm older now
I'll always need you here.

THE STARS THAT KNEW YOU

Change is coming for me
faster than I can run.
I cannot help but wonder
where has all the time gone?

Soon you'll be leaving for school,
a place that is states away.
I wish we could do this together
because it's always been that way.

I must confess I'm terrified
that we'll be strangers when you return.
But when I say this, you only smile and swear,
"We'll know each other forever. We're sisters."

LYRA WREN

After you left for college
I went and laid on your bedroom floor.
It had been picked apart,
pieces of it ripped away,
my favorite photo of us
missing from the wall.

I didn't realize how lonely I would be
knowing you aren't just down the hall.

"Come back," I start to whisper
grateful you aren't here to feel guilty
when my tears begin to fall.

THE STARS THAT KNEW YOU

I guess I just thought
that it would be me and you forever.

That we would always
live in the same house
and eat across from each other
at the same kitchen table.

It didn't cross my mind
that growing up meant
we would grow apart
to live our own lives.

I know that's just the way things are
but I never imagined it would be this hard.

LYRA WREN

Can we go to the end together?
Let's take it to the grave.
Our parents will leave too soon
and our children and lovers will come too late.

Let's dance among the stars
as we watch our eternity pass.
You were the first person I talked to
and I hope you'll be the last.

THE STARS THAT KNEW YOU

Watching your older sister leave home
is both pride and pain filled.
She's been by my side since the day I was born
and now that she's leaving it's hard not to mourn.

I told myself that she was only
a phone call away but when I see
the empty seat at the dinner table,
it's just not the same.

So to my older sister, I just wanted to say
that I'll always want you here
but I know you cannot stay.

And though I hate to say goodbye
to the childhood we've left behind,
I'll have your back forever
just like you've always had mine.

Section III: Stellae

The Latin Word for Stars.

We live together among the stars
and tell them about our story.

Our sisterhood and what that means,
a universal truth for all to see.

Sisterhood is a sacred bond
built with pinky promises and spilled blood.

We are a treasure trove of secrets
and oaths sealed tight.
Fortified by shared trauma and our endless fights.

It's a tie between souls that's impossible to undo.
Sisters are irreplaceable. I'll never find another you.

THE STARS THAT KNEW YOU

Pleiades is my favorite constellation
and I've never had to wonder why.
What's not to love about seven sisters
playing together up in the sky?

The eldest, Maia.
The youngest, Merope.
And all of those in between:
Electra, Alcyone, Taygete, Asterope, and Celaeno.

Each sister is unique but they are tied together
in all the ways that matter.

They will be with each other for all eternity
and I hope the same happens for you and me.

LYRA WREN

You are my worst enemy
and my greatest friend.
You've twisted the knife
and mended me up again.

On the outside it seems like a twisted bond
but maybe that's just how sisters love.

THE STARS THAT KNEW YOU

We've created a secret language
that only we can understand.
A single look saying what no words could.
An inside joke that makes our ribs ache
and the mere mention of a memory
that brings a smile to our faces.

Siblings are special.
We are different but our childhoods reflect each other
so we are the only ones who will ever get one another.

Being sisters means you'll peel
the rinds of your oranges
and while the smell of citrus
saturates the air,
you'll find yourself handing
over half for an equal share.
Because being siblings is
willingly going half hungry
to share in life's sweetness.

THE STARS THAT KNEW YOU

My sister and I screamed at each other again,
parting with wounded feelings.

It's only minutes later that
she comes back into my room,
eyes puffy from crying and voice hoarse.

We both sniffle in silence for a moment,
while she lingers by the bedroom door
before she asks, "Wanna get food?"

And suddenly I'm not mad anymore
so I just say, "Sure."

LYRA WREN

When it comes to my sister
I can never hold my anger for long.
The frigid feelings always melt away
as if they were never there at all.

We have wounded one another
far too often with bitter words
but forgiveness is ingrained in us.
That is sisterhood.

THE STARS THAT KNEW YOU

It's hard to explain to someone without siblings
that yes, we just had a screaming match.
We cried and said things we couldn't take back.

And yet, if one of us started to sing,
the others would join in without even thinking.

LYRA WREN

I don't trust many with my heart,
the pain too much to bear.
But I give it to my sister gladly
knowing she will handle it with care.

And though she throws me teasing jabs
that don't have any bite,
if someone were to come at me
she wouldn't hesitate to fight.

THE STARS THAT KNEW YOU

Our childhoods are so tangled
it would be impossible to undo.
But though our branches grow apart
I'm happy my roots are next to you.

We may bloom in different directions
but someone couldn't part us if they tried.
Because while we may seem different now,
we will never truly leave each other's sides.

Sometimes I pray that I will be the first
to return to stardust so I will never know
a life without you.

And maybe that's selfish but it's true.

THE STARS THAT KNEW YOU

I have no idea how I can be so close to someone
yet not recognize you at all.
But at the same time,
I knew you once and I know you now.

The same blood runs through our veins
but I can't seem to recall
the last time we had a late night talk
and spoke of things
we couldn't tell anyone else.

We have secrets that are buried
that we'll never tell each other.
And sudden truths spilled at the kitchen table
we will never tell another.

An only child asked me if I was afraid
that I would never experience unconditional love.
And what a silly question it was.

"I already know what it is to be loved.
I have my sisters. That is enough."

THE STARS THAT KNEW YOU

We've left our make believe worlds behind
with our childhoods attached.
But I often want to grab your hand in mine
and demand that we go back.

"Let's run away to the moon together," I plead.
"At least one more time."
I want to stay for an eternity,
playing pretend while we climb
each nook and crevice.

Searching for lost minutes
so I can make this moment last.
We can play tag and I'll chase you first
so please promise to follow me back.

I can daydream as much as I please
that we are small again
but the truth is right in front of me.
We are older now and our adventures on the moon
are now a distant reality.

LYRA WREN

We are sitting at our kitchen table
playing board games like we usually do,
poking fun at one another
and cracking childish jokes.

My heart begins to feel warm
and I press my hand to my chest.
I realize that everything I need is right here.
I fear I'll never be this happy again.

I wouldn't mind being born again
as long as you were still my sister.

Since the moment we were born
we've shared a last name.
And I didn't think about that changing
until you got engaged.

I choke down my tears each time
I picture your wedding day,
coming to terms with the fact that
your kids will always refer to me
as "my mom's *extended* family."

THE STARS THAT KNEW YOU

The nostalgia hits me hard some days,
forming a lump in my throat.

And I don't know how to swallow it down
and cope with the fact that
the most time I'll have spent with you in life is over.

There will be no more summers
filled with our girlish giggles.
No more make-believe lands
that only we could understand.

No waking up each morning
knowing you are home with me
because you live somewhere else now
and you're building your own family.

Sneaking into each other's rooms
is a thing of the past.
But there are so many nights that
I'd give anything to go back.

LYRA WREN

I miss the days of living in the same place
and playing in *our* backyard.
When the sand spilling from the hourglass
seemed like it would never move.

I'm happy we got to grow up together
but I wish it didn't have to end so soon.
And though I'd never say it to your face,
I'll say it here: I miss you.

THE STARS THAT KNEW YOU

Distance has pulled us apart
as growing up tends to do.
We are living our own lives now
so we don't get to talk as much as we used to.

But when we do see each other
and I hear her call my name,
I am just a girl playing
with her sisters again.

Special Acknowledgments

I. *To N,* who taught me compassion and how to laugh in life's roughest moments

II. *To S,* who taught me ambition and to never apologize for being who you are

III. *To A,* who taught me confidence and to pursue what you want in life

IV. *To the girls,* an entity and identity I could never live without

Acknowledgments

There are so many people to thank and gush about
that I needed a whole new page.

- Thank you to my mom who constantly inspires me, pushes
  me to follow my dreams and listens to me on my worst
  and best days. And for dealing with us when we complain
  about each other (sorry mom!)

- Thank you to my dad for supporting me in this journey
  wholeheartedly and for always encouraging me to pursue
  my creative ideas.

- Thank you to Keller for never complaining when I send
  you hundreds of new poems and for designing this book
  and my last.

- Thank you to my best friends and family who always encourage me and are the first to buy my books.

- Thank you to Maddie for editing this book and making sure it came out looking polished.

- Thank you to my followers and readers, I couldn't do this without all of you encouraging me and reminding me why I write. To bring comfort, compassion and understanding to my audience. You make me feel loved and heard. I hope I make you feel the same way.

About The Author

Lyra Wren is a poet and storyteller born and raised in Indiana. She's been a creative ever since she was a little girl whether that was doodling in the empty spaces of her homework or writing countless stories for her family to read. She has a bachelor's degree in studio art at Indiana University. When she isn't writing in the cafe of her local bookstore, Lyra spends much of her time painting, reading, enjoying the outdoors, curating spotify playlists and perusing astrological charts.

In 2021, Lyra began posting her poetry to TikTok and she has since grown her online following into a large supportive community. She strives to bring comfort, hope and understanding to her audience and make the world a place where people feel a bit less alone.

 *@poetrybylyra*

@canned.spaghettio

About The Book

The Stars That Knew You is a collection of poetry
touching on sisterhood and the curious complexities it brings.
Siblings are full of contradictions.
They know you, humble you and inspire you all in one breath.
Many people come and go, but they are the only ones
that stick with you for a lifetime.

It is split into three sections:
Solis, Lunae, and Stellae.
Each chapter deals with the different identities
that come with sisterhood.

For a few months, I was stuck on what I wanted
my next book to be about.
A common piece of advice for writers
is to write about what you love and know
and nobody fits that description more than my sisters.

While this book is an ode to my love for them,
it is also for all of those out there who have sisters.
Out of all the topics I write about,
my readers, by far, connect the most with my sister poetry.
I think that speaks to the importance of that relationship.

Also by Lyra Wren

The Lost Girls takes readers through the ups and downs of life.

This book is a collection of poems reminding people
to find joy in the journey and the little things.

It reminds us to engage with our emotions even when it hurts.

That life is about discovery and rediscovery
and that it's normal to feel lost.

Finding beauty in the day to day,
even when things feel adrift,
is a tremendous power.

Fireflies are not stars but it's still okay for us
to dream on them anyway.

(Cover and book design by Keller Makemson.)

Praise for *The Lost Girls*

"It's like lyra wren was able to bring out all of my thoughts in the most beautiful spot on way.

Allowing us to realize we are not alone with our feelings and experiences. This set of poetry helps you look into a scramble mind in a lovely manner.

A must read to understand one another."

— *LienRenders*

"This is one of the most beautiful and creative poetry collections i've ever read. i'm convinced she crawled inside of my brain and wrote down all of my thoughts then made poems out of it. i don't have the right words to explain how breathtaking this book is."

— *Mae Setrova*

"It's not an easy feat to tackle big topics in short-form writing and poetry, but Lyra is so talented... I highly recommend The Lost Girls to all women, all readers who care about women, and anyone who likes poetry...I will definitely be rereading this collection, and sharing more of Lyra's work in the future."

— *Hayley*

Made in the USA
Las Vegas, NV
15 December 2024